The Kingdom Driven Entrepreneur's Guide To Extraordinary Leadership

---

David A. Burrus

Foreword by

Shae Bynes and Antonina D. Geer

Co-Founders, Kingdom Driven Entrepreneur ™

The Kingdom Driven Entrepreneur's Guide to Extraordinary Leadership

ISBN 978-0989632232

Copyright 2013 by Kingdom Driven LLC
All rights reserved.

Published by Kingdom Driven Publishing
4846 N. University Drive #406
Lauderhill, FL 33351

Printed in the United States of America

All rights reserved. No portion of this book may be reproduced by any means - electronic, mechanical, photocopy, recording, scanning, or other - except for brief quotations in reviews or articles, without the prior written permission of the publisher. Your support of the authors' rights is appreciated.

Contents

Acknowledgements	1
Foreword	3
Introduction	5
Principle #1: Keep the Main Thing The Main Thing	7
Principle #2: Harness Your Shortcomings	18
Principle #3: Get Uncomfortable	26
Principle #4: Lead On Another Level	35
Principle #5: Position Yourself For A Shift	44
Principle #6: It's Lonely At The Top	53
Principle #7: Giving Your All	64
Conclusion	72
About The Author	74
Online Bonus Resources	75

Acknowledgments

There is no leadership if there is no followship. Yes, I just made up a word, but then again, leadership is often about making it up as you go. I want to take a moment to thank a few people who have been patient with me in life as I have "made it up" as I went.

Thank you to my Lord and Savior Jesus Christ for allowing me to do the things that He is allowing me to do in this season of my life. I have always dreamed of writing books and empowering people, I just never realized that that was not an original dream. It's the dream that you have had for me all of the time. You placed that dream in my heart 18 years ago, and it is finally coming to pass. Thank you for seeing me for who I am, and not for who I'm not.

To my amazing wife Tanisha Burrus who has been extraordinarily consistent with me while I've figured this "purpose thing" out. Thank you for not being impressed with any of this because you have always expected this and more from me. You keep me feeling loved and grounded, and I couldn't ask for anything more. I am still trying to show off for you. I'll never stop chasing you across the parking lot. (Wink Wink)

To Zion J. Burrus and Micah-Israel Burrus: It does something incredible for me to see you two making little books around the house with paper and staples. Thank you for making me feel like the "dad that can do anything". One day I hope to be that man that you think that I am. I love you boys from now to eternity.

To Shae Bynes and Antonina Geer: You two ladies have pushed me relentlessly, without even knowing it. Your passion for people, your drive, and your pursuit of excellence have rubbed off on me in ways that you will never understand. Whenever I say it, I mean it, I am honored to call you sisters, and even more honored to have been afforded the opportunity to write a book for the community that I proudly call my family – Kingdom Driven Entrepreneur. This is just the beginning of something amazing. Before you know it, we will able to afford our tents for our tent meetings. (Inside Joke)

To You, The Reader: There are millions of books that you could have chosen to read, and I am honored that you have chosen this book. I pray that it pushes you beyond the edge of ordinary into your rightful place as an extraordinary person, and leader. God bless.

Foreword

As a Kingdom Driven Entrepreneur you are called to serve your family, truly impact lives, and advance the Kingdom of God – and doing business God's way requires leadership.

Yes, you are called to be a leader in the marketplace. No matter who you are, where you've been, or what you've done to this point, God has given you extraordinary leadership potential. This book will encourage, inspire, and challenge you to access and embrace that potential to be the leader He has created you to be.

David A. Burrus shares wisdom which is grounded in the truth that you can only lead effectively when you follow God's blueprint. David shares scripture as well as memorable stories from his own leadership walk to bring to life the principles of extraordinary leadership.

As you're reading this book you will find encouragement to see the leader that God sees in you. You will be challenged to embrace who you are as well as who you are not in order to step into a new level of leadership that He's calling you to. You will recognize your unique God-given ability which will serve as a benefit to the many people who are in need and are awaiting your leadership.

If you're an active member of the Kingdom Driven Entrepreneur family, you know that Pastor Burrus is one of those visionaries who can find a leadership lesson in any situation – from changing a flat tire to breaking a pair of glasses. He relays these lessons in an engaging in an engaging and thought-provoking way. You are in for treat and will without doubt be blessed by the wisdom shared in the following pages.

This is a book that is designed to be studied prayerfully, not just read. We encourage you to read this guide to extraordinary leadership multiple times – each time from the lens of the various leadership roles you play in business, in your family, in your church or community. You serve a limitless God, and you can experience a new dimension of leadership in every area of your life!

> Shae Bynes and Antonina Geer
> Founders, Kingdom Driven Entrepreneur
> KingdomDrivenEntrepreneur.com

Introduction

I remember it like it was yesterday. It was in 1998 when I decided to become an extraordinary leader. I was 22 years old at the time, and I was about to make a leadership decision that would forever change the course of my life. I was living in Long Beach, California and I had decided that there were better opportunities for me back in the San Francisco Bay Area where I was from. I had very little money. I was living in a one room studio apartment with a microwave, a futon, a black and white television, and my clothes. It was a Monday afternoon when I decided that on the following Friday, I was going to take my pay check to purchase a used car, I was going to put as many of my belongings as would fit in the car, and I was going to move back to the Bay Area.

Friday morning came, and after spending all week researching used cars, I found one that I liked. It was a silver 1990 BMW coupe. I met with the owner, I purchased the car, and I went back home to load up my belongings. Because I didn't know much about cars, I took his word that the car was in good running condition, and based on the look and the sound, it was. I was well on my way, except I needed to stop to fill up the tank for the 6 hour journey ahead. I pulled into the gas station, filled up the tank, and went to start the car only to discover that the car would not start. I waited for five minutes and tried again, only to find that the car still wouldn't start. Houston, we have a problem. It was at that moment that I made the decision of my life.

I noticed that about 30 yards away was a Greyhound station, and at that moment I had to make a decision. I had to decide whether I was going to leave it all to start a new future, or stick around to repair what was in my past. Needless to say, I grabbed whatever I could out of that car, I left the keys in the ignition, and walked to the Greyhound station to catch a bus back to the Bay Area. Yes, I left that beautiful BMW at gas pump 6 in Long Beach, California, because I had too much to gain to be bound by a problem of my past.

Kingdom Driven Entrepreneur, as you are reading this book, it is my prayer that the extraordinary leader in you will stand up. I pray that you will encounter your own pump 6 experience. As you read this book, my desire is that God will use these words to cause you to walk away from any mentality or disposition that hinders you from walking into your purpose and your destiny. Get ready to embrace your next level as God's extraordinary leader.

Principle #1:
Keep the Main Thing the Main Thing

"One of the greatest ways to sabotage your own potential is to attempt to pursue a mission that you have not clearly identified."

As I have had the opportunity to interact with and pour into the lives of leaders, I have discovered a common thing that I believe separates an ordinary leader from an extraordinary leader. That thing is purpose; and more importantly, a clearly defined and clearly articulated purpose. Myles Munroe states in his book *Discovering the Kingdom* that where purpose is unknown, abuse is inevitable. When you have not clearly identified and articulated why someone or something exists, it is bound to be abused, misused, and misappropriated.

As we journey through this book in the pursuit of extraordinary leadership, it is vitally important that you understand that before you can effectively lead anyone or anything, you must first effectively lead yourself. That self-leadership begins with self-discovery. It begins with the ability to answer with great certainty the questions **who am I, and why am I here**.

While this is not a book about purpose, I deem it important to take a few moments to help some identify their purpose, and to help others confirm their purpose. Allow me to share with you these five simple ways that will help you identify your purpose:

1. Your purpose is often the thing that you would do for the rest of your life for free. It's that thing that you find absolute joy in doing, and that you could do all day everyday without any monetary compensation.

2. Your purpose is often the thing that agitates you and/or irritates you the most. It's that thing that haunts you to see it not being done, or to see it being done ineffectively or improperly. You were created in response to a problem in the earth.

3. Your purpose is often the thing that won't seem to leave you alone until you fulfill it. It's the thing that you think of at least once a day every day of the week. It's the book you are supposed to write or the music project that you are supposed to record. It's the business that you are supposed to start or that non-profit that you are supposed to found. It is the thing that consumes you.

4. Your purpose is the thing that others repeatedly tell you that you are good at. It's the things that you say or do that others have found value in.

5. Your purpose is the thing that seems to speak up for you, even when you aren't trying to bring it up. It's the thing that seems to always find its way into your conversations. Your purpose is a part of your DNA.

While there are countless other things that will help you identify your purpose, these five things will lead you down a successful path of discovery and understanding. Remember that your purpose is about who you are. It is the reason that you exist in the earth. Extraordinary leadership is about first following after the distinct purpose that you were created fulfill in the earth. You are an answer to someone's problem.

WHAT IS YOUR PERSONAL MISSION STATEMENT?

There is a very well-known hip hop artist named Shawn Carter (Jay-Z) who stated "I'm not a businessman, I'm a business man." That statement speaks volumes, as he is clearly identifying himself beyond the confines of an organization or a system. He is essentially stating that HE is the organization and system. While that can certainly be perceived metaphorically, there is a great deal of practicality to that statement as well. Practicality that I believe every leader should learn from and champion.

When you are flowing in the fullness of your potential and capabilities, you are an unstoppable machine. When you are following after your purpose, there is not another person who can compete with you being you. One of the greatest ways to sabotage your own potential is to attempt to pursue a mission that you have not clearly identified.

One of the first things that most great organizations do when laying the foundation of their institution is to identify their mission statement. A mission statement is simply the formal aims or values that govern the affairs of a particular company, organization, or individual. Most mission statements are one or two sentences that articulate the culture and aim of an organization. I am currently the founder and pastor of Hope City Church located in the lovely Central Texas area. When we were laying the foundation of the church, we aspired to create a one sentence mission statement that gave the listener a clear and concise overview of what our mission was. It's the big picture in one sentence. Our mission statement is *"We exist to seek the lost, teach the found, and send disciples, for the advancement of the Kingdom of God."* This one sentence clearly identifies who we are and why we are doing what we are doing. The benefit of a good mission statement is that it keeps the organization or individual on task, especially when decisions are being made.

I believe that every person should have their own individual mission statement. That may be a foreign concept to many, but there are so many benefits in knowing why you, as an individual, exist. Your personal mission statement will help you articulate your purposes and passions, and it will also keep you from pursuing endeavors that don't fit your personal mission. Do you know what you are here for? Have you identified who you are here to help and to empower? Have you identified what void you were created to fill? Allowing yourself to walk through that process of creating a personal mission statement will without doubt strengthen you as a leader.

Extraordinary leaders know who they are, why they exist, and when they are flowing in the fullness of their potential. They know these things because they have a personal mission statement, even when they haven't clearly articulated it or identified it. I am writing this because I want you ahead of the curve as a leader, and the most effective way to do that is through an assurance in knowing who you are, and why you exist. What is your personal mission statement?

REMEMBER THE ULTIMATE MAIN THING

Have you ever found yourself pursuing promotion or increase? Have you ever experienced what it's like to pursue a position or certain status? Perhaps you, like me, have spent time in the pursuit of wealth and/or material things. It is easy to make any one of these things the main thing, but that is slippery slope that has the potential to cause a great deal of spiritual and emotional damage. None of these things are as important or fulfilling as seeking and finding the ultimate main thing. So, what is that ultimate main thing?

Matthew 6:33 clearly defines what the main thing is, as well as the results of a people who passionately pursue the main thing. It states *Seek the Kingdom of God above all else, and live righteously, and He (God) will give you everything that you need.* He makes it quite clear that the benefits that we are looking for can be found and guaranteed when we adjust our pursuit to that of the Kingdom of God. If there were ever anything that distinguished a mediocre leader from an extraordinary leader, it is his ability to make the Kingdom of God his priority. God rewards those who diligently seek Him. As you are reading this, I charge you to sure up your vision and mission by allowing the ultimate main thing to take precedence over anything that you desire to see come to pass.

True leadership is true submission. In order to effectively lead on the level that God desires for you to lead on, you must first follow and submit on the level that requires brokenness and humility.

CREATE A PERSONAL BOARD OF DIRECTORS

I am honored to sit as a member of the board of directors for one of the most powerful Christian organizations of our time, Kingdom Driven Entrepreneur. I share this position with three other incredibly gifted leaders in their own right. What I have found fascinating about this particular board of directors is their commitment to the Kingdom Driven Entrepreneur vision and culture. However, what I find more interesting is that every one of the board members cares enough about the vision and direction of the organization to say the things that need to be said to the leaders of the organization, even when it is hard and uncomfortable. When we dissect what it is that makes these conversations work, and what it is that allows for egos to remain intact, it comes as a result of three very specific things:

1. The founders/leaders of the organization care more about being in the will of God than they care about being right.

2. The board of directors care more about the health of the organization than they do about protecting the leaders' egos.

3. Both the leaders and the board of directors want God's will to be manifested though the organization.

Those three things make for a winning combination, because at the end of the day, it is ultimately about God's will being manifested. As you can see, there are some very clear benefits to having a board of directors over your organization. They often see what you can't see. They, in many cases, have experienced things that you have yet to experience. Another major benefit is that they can help you make decisions that you would have to struggle to make alone. What is most important about an effective board of directors is that their responsibility is not to lead the organization, but they are commissioned to support the organization through counsel and direction.

Once you have completed your personal mission statement, I encourage and challenge you to assemble a personal board of directors. This is a group of 3-4 mature individuals you trust who will agree with you about your mission and will support you in your decision making, both as an individual and as a leader. You may already have a few individuals you lean on for counsel and direction in those tough times of decision making. I invite you to take those relationships a step further by asking them to officially serve on your personal board of directors. The point of making it official is so that they are aware of the fact that they are to hold you accountable for doing the things you have said are what God has called you to do. One of the things that separate ordinary leaders from extraordinary leaders is their desire and ability to be held accountable.

Be careful to appoint people who are spiritually mature, accountable themselves, trustworthy, and love you enough to be candid with you about you and your decision making. You don't need people who are too timid to be honest and transparent with you as there cannot be true growth and development to the degree that you need under those circumstances. Pray about whom it is that God would have you to select to be on your personal board of directors, and then pray about the timing in which you are to ask them. When you have selected your personal board of directors, schedule a consistent time that you can meet with them to pray with them, update them, and to hear any instruction or counsel from them that the Holy Spirit may give to them to deliver to you. One of the greatest benefits of a personal board of directors is their ability to help you keep the main thing that main thing. Extraordinary leaders are those that stay on task, no matter what storms, shifts, or seasons may hit their life.

COACHES AND MENTORS

What I have learned over the last two years of starting the Hope City Church is that you can never have enough insight and direction regarding your vision, mission, and goal. While books are one of the greatest tools and sources of pertinent information, there is something to be said about having a simple yet profound conversation with someone who has gone further than you have. To add to that, there is also a great wealth of knowledge that can be gained from those who have not gone further than you have, or have failed at what you are attempting to do. In many cases, their failing experiences are just what you need for your successful experiences. The difference between a coach and a mentor is that a mentor gives advice based on their wisdom, experience, and insight. Mentors freely give answers and solutions to the problems or questions at hand. Coaches, on the other hand, assist you in discovering the answer or solution to the problem. Coaches walk you through a systematic process of discovery and development. Both coaches and mentors are vital to your development as a leader.

Extraordinary leaders are teachable. They are fully aware that they do not have all of the answers. One of the things that keep leaders from experiencing the fullness of their calling is their inability to submit to a coach or a mentor who can push them to their next level. In other instances, many don't realize that they need a coach or a mentor who will push them. I have had the opportunity to coach and mentor leaders, and I have had the opportunity to be coached and mentored as a leader. There is absolutely no substitute for the boost that is experienced in a coach/mentor/mentee relationship. If you are reading this, it is probably because you are currently a leader, or feel like there is leadership potential in you waiting to be birthed. I advise you to pray and ask God to send you a coach and/or a mentor that will push you to your next level. Your vision will thank you for it.

TAKE ACTION

1. Create your personal mission statement.

2. Seek God for direction on who should be on your personal board of directors – and reach out to them in the appropriate timing.

3. Ask God to send you a coach or mentor who can help you achieve what God has called you to do as a leader.

Principle #2
Harness Your Shortcomings

"If you are ever going to lead in an extraordinary way, you have to learn to champion who you are, and be at peace with who you are not."

Have you ever played The Comparison Game in your head? You know The Comparison Game, don't you? It's the game that you play when you see someone who "appears" to have more pulchritude, more ingenuity, and more things than you do. The Comparison Game is the conversation that you have in your head when they walk in the room that causes you to say "I am not _____ enough to hold a conversation with them." Or the thing that makes you say "I am too _____ to even approach them". Or, the conversation that you have in your head that says "I will never be able to _____ like they do it".

The Comparison Game is the conversation that you have secretly in your head that talks you out of everything that God has talked you into by highlighting your shortcomings over your strengths. As you are reading this, can you think of a time that you have played the comparison game with yourself? How did that work for you?

If you are ever going to lead in an extraordinary way, you have to learn to champion who you are, and be at peace with who you are not. In order to be at peace with who you are not, you have to take an honest assessment of your strengths as well as your weaknesses. For the next few chapters, I am going to highlight the life of a chief tax collector in the Bible named Zacchaeus (Luke 19:1-10). For the sake of this book, I will commonly refer to him as Zack. While it never refers to Zack as a leader of people, and nothing else is said about his life outside of this encounter in Luke 19:1-10, he is personally one of my favorite leadership examples in the Bible. You will see why as you journey on through this book.

One of the first things that we learn about Zack is that he had shortcomings, literally. It states in Luke 19:3 *He tried to get a look at Jesus, but he was too short to see over the crowd*. What we will later discover is that in spite of his short stature, he did not allow that to hinder him from seeing Jesus. Zack discovered something about himself that every leader must at some point discover about himself to shift from ordinary to extraordinary. Zack discovered that he was not his stature. He discovered that he had a height problem, not a destiny problem. Zack was able to decipher between what he could not change and what he could change. While the Bible doesn't give any clear indication into the mindset of Zack, one could only assume that he made a decision not to play The Comparison Game. Zack decided that his destiny was a much greater destiny than spending his life staring at the backsides of those who didn't want what he wanted badly enough.

When you discover who you are as a person and as a leader, then who you are *not* will have absolutely no precedence in your decision making. When you discover who you are, then you can harness who you are not, and cause it to work to your advantage. Allow me to show you how.

STOP COMPLAINING ABOUT IT....DO SOMETHING!

As an extraordinary leader, you must know that who you are not is just as valuable to you as who you are. We started this book discussing purpose, and what we discovered is that *purpose speaks to direction*. When you have discovered who you are in God as a leader, that revelation will undoubtedly steer you in directions where your assets and leadership ability will be most effective. Discovering who you are not as a leader keeps you from pursuing endeavors and opportunities that do not speak to your purpose.

In Luke 19:3, Zack had one of two choices to make based on his shortcoming. One possible choice was to spend his time complaining about how everyone else was taller than him, or how everyone else had an advantage over him. He could have spent his time allowing who he was not to define who he was, and who he would ultimately become. Whether you consider yourself a leader or not, I charge you to make up your mind that you will not spend another valuable moment rehearsing your shortcomings. Why? Because you perfect what you practice. Zack chose to make a different decision, and it's one that I hope that you and I choose to make whenever we are confronted with our shortcomings. He decided to use who he was not as motivation to drive him to become who he would ultimately become.

I know that you have shortcomings, but what are you going to do about them? When my wife and I married in 2003, I weighed 150 pounds. Sometimes I look back at the pictures, and I cannot believe that I was ever that small. When my son was born just 9 months after our wedding, I weighed a little over 200 pounds. In just 9 months I gained over 50 pounds and I have not been able to lose those extra pounds ever since. I have tried all types of lose weight quick fads, but none of them have had any lasting effects. As I am writing this, I am on day one of a serious change of lifestyle. I decided to eat better and to implement exercise into my daily routine. I know that this seems to have nothing to do with leadership, but it does. It is about me taking ownership of who I am not, and deciding that I am going to move toward becoming who I know that I can be.

I am merely doing what Zack did. He took his shortcoming, and he leveraged it by using it as motivation to go achieve his destiny. Extraordinary leaders are those who use their disadvantages to their advantage. I know that there are areas in your life that you feel like as a person and/or as leader, you are missing the mark. What are you going to do about it? How long are you going to complain about the butts that are in your face keeping you from seeing Jesus?

How long will you harp over who is in front of you blocking you from achieving what you desire? When you are an extraordinary leader, you allow your desires to push you past that which tried to hold you back. As you read this, I pray that there is a fire rising inside of you that will lead you to make the decision to go after it by any means necessary.

THE BUTT MENTALITY

You may be thinking "Ok, enough with the butt talk!" but I am determined to press into this issue to ensure that you get this. Zack had many of the same problems that you and I have as people, and especially as leaders. His problem was that there were too many butts in his face for him to see Jesus. Your problem and my problem is often that there are too many "buts" in our face to see Jesus. You know the "I would but…" conversations that we have with ourselves. Allow me to preface my next statement by saying that what I am about to say is offensive, and it is meant to be. Are you ready? As long as you are comfortable making decisions based on the "buts" that are in your face, your climate will never change, and you will always live in the face of frustration.

Your will must change before your situation changes. Extraordinary leaders do what Zack did; they align their will with God's divine destiny for their life, and they adjust their lifestyles accordingly. Zack was in no way satisfied with his current situation, and he refused to adopt a butt mentality as the norm for his life. The root of the "but" is fear. It is the fear of failure, and in many cases, the fear of success. It's often easier to settle in the seat of mediocrity, than to soar on the wings of success. Fear has the potential to destroy your destiny one excuse at a time. As leaders, it is imperative that on every level and in every phase of our leadership, that we eliminate the "buts" in our lives. Your shortcomings do not have to define your destiny. You give your life permission to do and to be what it will be, and you do so by the way that you respond to the negativity that comes to distract you from realizing your destiny.

RECOGNIZE YOUR DESTINY MOMENT

I am reminded of a story that took place in South Africa about a mule that ended up in a ditch while he was traveling. The ditch was far too deep for him to climb out of. The mule's owner did everything that he could to rescue the mule from this dire situation, but to no avail. Finally he came to the conclusion that the only thing left to do was to bury the mule alive. He left and returned with the tools, only to find the mule winded and defeated from his attempts to climb out of the hole. The owner reluctantly began throwing dirt on the mule in an attempt to bury it alive. What he discovered was that the more dirt that he threw in, the more the mule would shake the dirt off of his back. The more dirt that the mule would shake off, the more dirt he had under his feet. Finally after a couple of hours of filling the hole, the helpless mule had enough dirt under his feet to step out of the hole onto level ground. I believe that the owner and the mule both recognized a destiny moment.

Romans 8:28 reminds us that as extraordinary leaders, no matter how many "buts" we face, it is going to work out for our good when we love God and when we are leading according to his plan for our lives. I dare you to shake the shortcomings in your life off, and to stand on them, even as the mule stood on his. The dirt was designed to suffocate him and to bury him alive, and the enemy of your vision desires to use your shortcomings to suffocate your vision, and to bury it alive. I challenge you to make a declaration today that what once held you bound will become a stepping stool to your next blessed place as an extraordinary leader.

I want to make you a promise, and you can hold me to it. I promise you that your "Yes Lord" will take you much further as a leader than your "But, Lord..." will ever take you. Your complete surrender to His will for your life in spite of what you think you are able and unable to do is the scholarship to your next dimension in Him. He has called you to live, love, and lead on another level, but that level can only be obtained when you allow the God who called you to be more powerful than the enemy who only seeks to hinder you. He knew that you had issues before He called you to lead. Your issues, your shortcomings, and your baggage do not intimidate Him. If God isn't concerned about it, why should you be? If you are going to be an extraordinary leader, it will require a God's eye view and perspective on who He says that you are.

TAKE ACTION

1. Reflect on a time you played The Comparison Game. Write down the thoughts you had and the action you took (or didn't take) as a result of those thoughts.

2. Read the story about Zacchaeus in Luke 19:1-10.

3. Take a written inventory of what you consider to be your shortcomings as well as what you consider to be your strengths. Are there things in your personal, business, or ministry life that God has called you to do, but you're too focused on your shortcomings to move forward? Take note of those things.

4. How do you think God sees you based on what you've read in the Word of God or what He has shared with you? Write it down.

5. Commit to one thing you're going to do differently, starting TODAY, using your shortcoming as a stepping stool to move forward.

Principle #3:
Get Uncomfortable

"There is no comfort zone in extraordinary leadership."

One afternoon while I was in the airport in North Carolina preparing to head back to my home in Texas, I witnessed something that really opened my eyes to what true genuine leadership looks like. There was a gentleman in front of me who had the most beautiful Louis Vuitton carry-on luggage. I watched him as he placed his luggage on the conveyer belt at security to go through the scanner. I must admit that I did what the average individual without Louis Vuitton luggage would do; I immediately began to covet his luggage. As funny as it sounds, I really did, for those 10 minutes he was in front of me in line, imagine myself rolling through the airport with that same Louis Vuitton carry-on that he had. I was so enthralled with the luggage, I watched his entire security process like a weirdo stalker. He was in such a hurry once he got to the other side of security and when he grabbed his expensive Louis Vuitton carry-on luggage, it snagged on something on the conveyer belt. As a result, the bag ripped wide open right there on the conveyer belt; only to expose that it was a knock off Louis Vuitton bag that I had been coveting all of that time.

I have encountered far too many leaders who are much like this Louis Vitton bag. They appear authentic until they get caught up in the issues of life, and then their lack of authenticity is exposed for everyone to see. It doesn't have to be that way. When God created you, He commissioned you as a prototype leader. That means that there is not one who has come before you, neither will there ever be one who comes after you who has your exact assignment, commission, and destiny. You are the prototype. You are a one of a kind leader. Extraordinary leadership is about the ability to accept the reality that there are no templates and/or blueprints that you can draw inspiration from, other than the Holy Spirit Himself.

EXTRAORDINARY RESULTS REQUIRE EXTRAORDINARY MEASURES

Zack, in Luke chapter 19:1-10, found himself in a quandary. He understood that if he was going to experience Jesus in this divine encounter, he was going to have to create a way to see Jesus. This impasse that Zack found himself confronting was the catalyst for the pioneer that was always residing within him. It compelled him to take extraordinary measures in order to experience extraordinary results. Moments like that in a leader's life are divinely assigned to call forth the creativity in the leader. They distinguish the ordinary from the extraordinary. What do you do when you face obvious adversity and conflict as a leader?

I submit to you that Zack was on to something. Luke 19:4 states that *he ran ahead and climbed a sycamore tree.* The thing that caused him to be successful in his pursuit of Jesus was his swift decision to get ahead and to get higher. Out of all of the people who were there crowding Jesus, Zack was the only one who made the decision to go ahead and to go higher. Let's take a closer look at why this is significant in the life of a leader:

1. *He went ahead.* Zack realized that if he was going to maximize this God encounter that he had to get ahead of the crowd. Extraordinary leaders must have the ability to move beyond the trend, and to become the trendsetter and the trailblazer. He understood that there was no possible way that he was going to experience the shift from within the crowd, so he made the conscious decision to run apart from the crowd to better position himself.

2. *He went higher.* Zack realized that the thing keeping him from seeing Jesus was his current level, so he forced himself to go higher. For you, the thing that may be keeping you from experiencing the fullness of God in your life is not lack of will, but rather lack of level. You have to think higher, expect higher, and live in a higher dimension of expectation. Low thinking yields low results.

3. *He was okay with looking foolish.* Pioneering new moves, shifts, and trends requires looking

like a fool in the eyes of those who have no discernment or vision. When God gives you a vision, it often requires you looking like a fool on paper, and a hero when it comes to pass. You have to be willing to suffer looking like a fool to experience the fullness of who God has called you to be.

There is no comfort zone in extraordinary leadership. It is going to require you to make uncomfortable decisions and to make equally uncomfortable moves. It will require you to live in dimensions of faith that the average person, or leader for that matter, is just not required to live. I challenge you to run ahead and to climb higher.

LEADING WITHOUT A CLUE

It is absolutely okay to not know what you are doing. And while we are on the subject, it is okay to not know what the end result is going to look like. You feel better now, don't you? I am a living witness that you can waste countless minutes, hours, days, months, and even years waiting on the details of a vision that are never coming. If you are waiting on the details, or you are waiting on the stars to be perfectly aligned before you move on it, you are wasting precious time. The Lord instructed Abraham, in Genesis 12:1, to "Go to the land that I will show you".

What kind of directions are those? What kind of navigation system is the Holy Spirit, if He is giving instructions like "Go, and I will show you when you have arrived"? What? Think about it. God commissioned Abraham to lead His people out of the enemy's hands, and the only instructions that He gave him was to head out and they would discuss the details later. How would you fair under those conditions? Interestingly enough, Abraham did as he was commanded. So, what did Abe have that we don't have? Nothing. In fact, it is safe to say that we have an even greater advantage because we have Holy Spirit living inside of us to navigate us.

I want you to place a bookmark in the book on this page for a second and grab your Bible because I want to take you on a 3 minute field trip. I want you to thumb through the book of Exodus, and notate how many times you read "Moses said to the Lord", or "The Lord said to Moses". Note how many times it states "The Lord replied to Moses". Take a few minutes to do that now. I will be here when you return.

Did you see that? Do you know why those phrases occurred so frequently in Exodus? It's because Moses was called to lead, but he didn't have a clue what he was doing. His effectiveness as a leader was in his ability to identify what he didn't know, and his ability to remain in the face of the God who was all-knowing. You not knowing what you are doing is not an excuse for you not to lead. Just as a pilot has to stay in constant communication with the control towers, a Kingdom Driven Entrepreneur who is an extra-ordinary leader has to stay in constant communication with the Holy Spirit.

BUILD WHAT? FOR WHAT?

There was a pretty famous guy in the Bible named Noah, and one day the Lord approached him with a small proposition. God advised Noah that He was about to send a flood on the earth to destroy all of civilization and that Noah was to build an ark for the flood that would house his family and two of every kind of creature on the earth. The odds are that you are familiar with the story of Noah's Ark, and Noah was one of the first Bible characters introduced to you as a child. As a result, this story probably doesn't really have much of an impact on you anymore because it is so familiar to you. For Noah, it wasn't a familiar story. He was living that moment in real time.

Consider this: mankind had never experienced a flood before, so there was no need for an ark prior to this moment in time. Noah had never seen an ark (nor a flood) in his entire life, and yet God was asking him to build one. I can just hear Noah now, saying under his breath, "You want me to build a what? For a what? What?" Noah wasn't the last person that God required to build something unusual for something unusual.

Perhaps you are reading this and contemplating the ark that God has required you to build for the flood that you have never experienced before. When God commissions you to pioneer a work, He is doing so because He desires to make you the blueprint and the prototype. The downside of it all is that there leaves no room for speculation. You have to live with your ear to the voice of the Holy Spirit. The good side of it all is that there leaves no room for speculation. You have to live with your ear to the voice of the Holy Spirit.

I must again reiterate that it is okay to not know what you are building, how you are building it, or what the end result is going to be. Take rest in knowing that the only one confused in the matter is you. God knows exactly what He is doing. It is in that instance that you must take rest in knowing that your most effective leadership moments will come as a result of you being in direct communication with the Holy Spirit.

DON'T ASK FOR THE OPPORTUNITY THAT YOU ARE TO CREATE

As I am writing this, I am reflecting on a moment in my life that really changed the game for me. It was 1999, and I was a single Christian man living in my hometown of the San Francisco Bay Area. I was very new to ministry, but had a sense that God would one day use me mightily to reach the lost for Christ. It was around that time that I listened to a CD that revolutionized my life. It was a recording of a local pastor by the name of Horacio Jones, and he and his wife were teaching a relationship seminar on marriage. While the information that he was sharing was impactful, that wasn't what really grabbed me. What grabbed me was the fact that he and his wife were teaching as a team and were equipping couples to live out the richness that God intended for their marriages to be. I was blown away. I played that CD over and over again until it eventually wore out. That one moment and that simple CD set me on a path and a course that led me to this very moment in time.

About 11 years ago, before my wife and I were married, we began teaching relationship seminars on a small scale. One of the things that we realized is that there are far too few church leaders who are willing to invest the time or the financial resources to teach on the topic (let alone have an outsider come in and teach on it). After years of compiling research and waiting on opportunities for us to share the research, we finally came to the conclusion that we were going to have to create the opportunity that we were waiting to be given to us. It was in 2006 that we started the Passion Summit Relationship Seminars. God is still using this venue to strengthen singles and couples alike in the area of Christian relationships. But what if we were still waiting around for an opportunity to do and to be what God requires of us? Imagine how frustrated we would be now!

Are you waiting on someone to give you an opportunity that you were destined to create? Pioneering means that you will build your own door frame, build your own door, place that door on the hinges, and walk through the door that you have created yourself. There are some of you who are reading this who are not called to pioneer and create a space for God to use you in. There are others of you who are reading this, and the Holy Spirit is speaking to you about taking the lead in certain areas of your life.

In case you haven't read the first few chapters of Genesis, we serve a very creative God. He has the capacity to create anything through anyone that He pleases. I charge you today to examine your heart. If you are waiting because the Holy Spirit has you waiting, by all means wait. But, if you know that God is ready to use you to pioneer a new work, and you are hesitating, don't let another day go by without operating in the dimension that you were called to operate in. If it doesn't exist, start it. If it does exist, improve it. Whatever you do, do not be afraid to pioneer something that you have never seen before. If God has called you to do it, He will see you through it.

TAKE ACTION

1. If God has called you to build an ark in your life, business, or ministry, seek God about the first (or the next best step) for you to take.

2. Consider what you may be waiting for someone else to create. Has God spoken to you about creating it? If you're unsure, ask Him!

Principle #4:
Lead on Another Level

"Operating at another level may mean you disrupt the system of those around you."

It was a sunny Sunday afternoon, and I had just settled into my seat on the airplane and was ready to get back home. To give you a little bit of history about me and airplanes, prior to this I had flown countless times before. In fact, one of my first memories of ever being on an airplane is the time when I was around nine or ten years old, and I took a 45 minute flight from Oakland, California to Los Angeles, California by myself. That's right. My mother put me on an airplane by myself to fly to Southern California to spend time with family. I am sharing this simply to point out that I have a great deal of experience flying and what happened this particular Sunday is quite unusual.

I'd sat down in my window seat and strapped my seatbelt on as I routinely do when I am flying. Shortly after that, a husband and wife filled the middle and aisle seat that was located directly next to me. Suddenly, the most overwhelming feeling of fear and anxiety came over me. I was sweating and shaking. I attempted to pray, but to no avail. Finally (and frantically) in a fit of desperation, I asked if the husband that was seated on the aisle seat next to me would switch seats with me. He reluctantly agreed to switch seats, and when he did I felt my anxiety level decrease with every passing moment. It was at that moment that I discovered that I had an enemy called claustrophobia that I needed to overcome. If you are not familiar with claustrophobia, it is simply a fear of tight or enclosed spaces. It is something that I still pray about, and am still fighting to overcome this very day. So, what does my claustrophobia have to do with becoming an extraordinary leader? In reality, it has everything to do with it. Here's how.

In Luke 19, I believe that Zack was experiencing spiritually what I experienced on that airplane that afternoon. Spiritual claustrophobia. It's that feeling that you get when you are no longer comfortable living in the box that you have created, or that others have created for you to live in -- the box of mediocrity and/or complacency. What I needed at that very moment was a shift. The shift wasn't about me being able to walk around freely, as mobility is limited in an airplane. My shift was about knowing that my movement was not limited to anyone else's willingness to allow me to move. It was about knowing that I wasn't bound by anyone else's actions.

Are you suffering from your own spiritual claustrophobia? Perhaps you feel it in your career, or in your ministry, or just in your own personal walk. The real question is what are you willing to do about the box that you are in?

One of the keys to becoming an extraordinary leader is to discipline yourself to lead from another level. What led to Zack's success was not just that he got ahead of the crowd, but more importantly, it was his ability to get above the crowd by climbing into the sycamore tree. You cannot lead on another level without changing your perspective. You cannot change your perspective without being intentional about exposing yourself to things that are on a level that you are not currently on. Next level leadership must be intentional. As I reflect back to my experience on the airplane, it was my persistence in making the shift that liberated me from the tight space that held me captive.

Operating at another level may mean that you disrupt the systems of those that are around you. Keep in mind that when God has called you to lead on another level, everyone and everything around is also divinely designed to support you. The sycamore tree had no choice. It was predestined and preapproved to serve Zack as he pursued his next level.

LEADING THROUGH EXCELLENCE

There is a wonderful leadership moment that we can draw from that is found in Matthew 14:13-21 where Jesus took two fish and five loaves of bread and fed five thousand men, not including women and children. What I find most intriguing about this moment in history is that among all other things, Jesus taught us how to operate in excellence. When we talk about excellence, we are simply talking about doing the very best with what you have. Jesus had only two fish and five loaves of bread, but He never viewed it as lack. He always viewed it as increase. He was about to do the very best with what He had. The Bible states that He broke the bread and divided it. Excellence -- He made what He had work, and work well.

Extraordinary leadership is not about having every resource available to you, but it is about maximizing the resources that are available to you. If God has called you and placed you in a leadership position, you are already starting out with enough. You have the calling of God on your life. God would never give you a vision that He has not already made provision for. It is your responsibility to maximize what He has given you. Zack didn't have the height that he needed to see Jesus, but he had the legs that he needed to get ahead of the crowd, and the tree that he needed to get above the crowd. Don't waste another valuable moment complaining about the sycamore trees that are in your life to elevate you to your next dimension of leadership.

The thing that separated Zack from the rest of the crowd was his ability to operate in excellence. It was his ability to use what he had available to him to achieve a greater goal and purpose. Zack stood out from the crowd because he was higher than the crowd -- literally. He'd intentionally positioned himself above the place that was hindering him from his destiny moment. Jesus would have overlooked Zack had he never made the adjustment to go higher. He would have never gone higher had he not been operating in excellence. He would have never been able to flow in the level of excellence that he did had he not had a revelation of his resources. Your ability to operate as an extraordinary leader is contingent on your ability to identify the divinely appointed resources that are at your disposal.

My prayer is that as you are reading this, God is revealing to you the specific resources that He has made readily available to you that will assist you in leading on your next level. What is your sycamore tree? What are you willing to use to lead on the next level? For some their sycamore tree may be a bad experience. That may be the thing that motivates a person run ahead and to climb higher. For someone else it may be the desire to help someone else. For Zack, his motivation was to have a deeper relationship with God. That is what motivated him to go further and higher.

LEAD THROUGH INNOVATION

The definition of the word duplication is *to be exactly like something else*. Contrary to the word duplication is the word innovation, which means *to begin or introduce something new*. In leadership there must be both duplication and innovation. What's concerning is that as I view the landscape of leadership in my immediate sphere of influence, it appears that I am seeing more duplicates than originals. This concerns me simply because when God has called you to innovate and you choose to be a carbon copy of someone else, you are essentially telling God that He is not creative enough to do anything new through you.

True leadership is just as much about innovation as it is about duplication. On one hand you want to ensure that you are multiplying yourself and cultivating leaders who have your leadership DNA. On the other hand, you also want to make sure that you are being creative and innovative in the way that you lead yourself and others. No two leaders are exactly the same. No two scenarios will require the same exact leadership responses. There will inevitably come moments in time where your leadership response must be unique, innovative, creative, and specific to that specific situation. It is in these leadership moments that God will impress on you to do something like run ahead of the crowd and climb into a sycamore tree. Your ears must be in tune with His voice, and your heart receptive enough to obey.

The God who created you also breathed life into you by way of His Spirit. The very Spirit that formed you, and is breathing in you, is the same Spirit that created everything with His words. As a leader, you have access to that same creative power and ability. You are by nature an innovator. In fact, the very breath in your body is an indicator that you are a living breathing pulsating walking bundle of creativity and innovation. It is better to be a great original than a cheap copy any day.

The problem with innovation is that there is a lack of any real reference point. I am most certain that to those around him, Zack looked like an absolute fool running and climbing into the tree. Remember that he was ahead of the crowd. There were undoubtedly others who were already near the tree and had no clue why this weirdo just ran top speed up and into the tree. As an extraordinary leader, you will not always be understood because innovation calls for great misunderstanding and scrutiny. People can rarely handle what they do not understand. You cannot afford to take your cues from people because very few have heard what God has given you in private. Don't allow the opinions of others to hinder your innovation. You were called to live and lead outside of the box. Never settle for a lower level just to satisfy people.

LEAD WITH PURE PURSUITS

There is something to be said about why Zack climbed into the tree on that day and at that moment. There are some who may have done it in order to be noticed by those who were around. There are others who may have done it to be viewed as a trailblazer, or as an innovator. There are surely others who would have done it just to get the attention of Jesus as He walked by. There was nothing self-promoting about what Zack did in that moment. The truth is that his pursuit was always that he might see Jesus. He wanted a deeper understanding and revelation of who Jesus really was. What we discover after reading further into that text is that Jesus fulfilled his desires, and even more...so much so that the people around Jesus were jealous.

The motivation for innovation should never be about what others will think about you. When your desire is to see God manifested in your endeavors, innovation becomes a byproduct. Please know that you cannot do anything that is innovative and out the box without it being noticed by those around you. However, what is even more important is that anything innovative and out the box you do to get to Jesus will move His heart with adoration and compassion. Your innovation goes a long way with the Holy Spirit, and with man. You cannot afford to have your motives tainted by self-ambition. Purify your pursuit and God will undoubtedly respond with grace and favor.

TAKE ACTION

1. Reflect on whether you're suffering from spiritual claustrophobia in any area of your life – personal or business/ministry. If so, write down how this spiritual claustrophobia is affecting your ability to boldly pursue what God has called you to. Also consider and write down what you're willing to do differently to bust through that box.

2. Are you taking full advantage of the resources that God has already made available to you?

 Take inventory of your resources and make note of any that are under-utilized and determine how best you can use them to take you to the next level of leadership.

Principle# 5:
Position Yourself For the Shift

"One of the greatest mistakes that a leader could ever make is to attempt to realize a grand vision before fulfilling the small persistent steps that it takes to do so."

There is something to be said about a person who would climb into a tree to get a better vantage point for any situation. That is exactly what Zack did in Luke 19:1-10. This wasn't just any parade going by, and it certainly wasn't just any old tree that he climbed into.

The sycamore tree has great significance, particularly as it relates to extraordinary leadership. While there isn't much said about what other types of trees were available for Zack to climb into, it is no coincidence that he chose to climb into this particular tree. What is interesting and significant about the sycamore tree of that day is that they were generally located at intersections. This means they had direct access to the north, south, east, and west. Can you see why the sycamore tree was so significant to Zack, in this pivotal moment in his life?

Picture it. He desires to see Jesus, and he knows that he may only have one chance. The crowd around Christ is prohibiting him from encountering the one man who can change his life. Zack decided that if he was ever going to experience the Christ, he had to get ahead of the move. He ran ahead of the parade and positioned himself in a sycamore tree so that no matter what direction Christ was coming from or leaving in, he would be positioned to experience His glory. Whether Christ was moving north, south, east, or west, Zack was in position to see Him come, and see Him go. There is a great deal to learn from this one moment in time. As an extraordinary leader, it is vitally important to position yourself for the shift. You must live in a constant state of preparation, so that you are available when new moves and shifts take place in your sphere of influence, or at the prompting of the Holy Spirit.

    I recall going on fishing trips with my aunt as a 9 and 10 year old child. I remember us sleeping in our fishing clothes the night before because we didn't want to waste valuable time getting dressed, because we would have to leave before the sun rose in the morning. We were, in essence, positioning ourselves for the shift. We stayed ready so that we didn't have to get ready. This is what extraordinary leadership is about. It is about positioning yourself for the shift. I encourage you to climb high into your spiritual sycamore tree, so that as you lead, you can flow with the moves and the shifts of the Holy Spirit. That is leadership at its finest.

POWER IN YOUR PLIABILITY

    If I had to use one word to describe leadership, that word would be heart. When we think of leading with heart, we commonly refer to the aspect of leadership that requires courage and bravery. While that is a vital aspect of what it means to lead with heart, there is an even deeper aspect. In Psalm 37:4 we are reminded to *delight thyself in the Lord, and He will give you the desires of the heart*. I believe that this principle is critical, and is one that should be grasped by leaders as early as possible. There is so much in this scripture that speaks to the life of the extraordinary leader. Let's take a closer look.

The psalmist implies that the way that we experience the fullness of the blessings that God has for us is for Him to be delighted by our lifestyles. It is, in fact, for Christ to find delight in us. But what does it really mean by delight? The word delight derives from the Hebrew word *anag*, which when translated means to be *soft or pliable*. If we were to take that a bit deeper, we would understand that to be pliable means to be *soft enough to bend freely or repeatedly without breaking*. Essentially what God is saying is "When your heart is able to bend and to form around the plans that I have for you, and when it is pliable enough to flex in any condition that I send you into, I can trust you enough to bless you."

Extraordinary leaders are those who lead with hearts that are pliable enough to bend at God's will, without breaking under the pressure of the circumstance. They are leaders who have a clear understanding that they are on assignment to fulfill God's will through whatever facet He has assigned them to lead in. Pliable leadership is about yielding your will to the will of the Lord. It is that same pliable heart that prompted Paul to confess in Philippians 4:11 that it didn't matter whatever state he found himself in, he would be content. It is that same pliable heart that prompted Zack to make the necessary adjustments to see the Christ even if that meant risking his reputation by climbing into the sycamore tree. It is this type of heart that lends itself to blessing. God favors leaders who lead with hearts that are pliable. He favors leaders who are intentional about seeking the Kingdom agenda first, over any agenda or ambition that they may ever have.

As you are reading this, and whether you currently consider yourself a leader or not, take some time to examine your heart. Allow God to search you as a person, and search you as a leader. I believe that one of the greatest weapons that the enemy uses against leadership is an impure heart and impure motives. Is your heart bent towards God's plan and will for your life as a person, and as a leader? Many leaders have fallen at the hands of their own impure motives and agendas. Those motives and agendas start in the heart, and end in scrutiny. Transparency with God (and being honest with yourself) will lead to a pliable heart, and a pliable heart is the ultimate positioning force for the favor of God as a leader. When you make His will your priority, He will make your success His priority. He is looking to give you the desires of your heart, and He is going to do so through His favor.

SCAVENGER HUNT LEADERSHIP

Have you ever been on a scavenger hunt? A scavenger hunt is a game played with two or more people. One person (or a group of people) chooses a particular area to play, and they set up different check points throughout the play area. In many cases, there are prizes obtained at these check points. A list of clues is provided to the contestants, and the person that hits all of the checkpoints and ends up at the finish line first is declared the winner. The key point of the scavenger hunt is for a person or a team to carefully follow directions and clues that lead them to their destination. Several small clues and small checkpoints lead to the ultimate checkpoint, and the victory for the person or team who finishes first.

Extraordinary leadership is about being diligent to the tasks at hand. Much like a scavenger hunt, being an effective leader has everything to do with your ability to flow one step at a time, and to accomplish one small goal at a time. One of the greatest mistakes that a leader could ever make is to attempt to realize a grand vision before fulfilling the small persistent steps that it takes to do so. It is the equivalent of having a puzzle that you want to enjoy the fullness of without going through the process of putting the pieces together.

There was a time in my life when I was struggling with fulfilling a certain aspect of the vision that God had given me to fulfill. I remember sitting down in frustration asking God what I was missing. I remember saying "Lord, I am confused. I don't know what to do next. What is my next step?" I remember hearing Him say to me in a very calm and clear voice, "Do the last thing that I told you to do". Yikes. My problem was that I wanted a next step without having completed the last step. Have you ever been in that situation? Have you ever been so frustrated with the lack of clarity of vision, that you just begin "going and doing" without "knowing"? What I am going to say next is sobering and liberating all at the same time. *Just because you can't clearly see the whole vision does not mean that you don't have vision.* It also doesn't mean that you are not to move forward.

Sometimes God gives you the pieces of the puzzle without showing you the box. Sometimes He will instruct you to start "it", without you really knowing what the "it" is that you are starting. The vision rarely comes with the details. Your responsibility and mine is to fulfill the vision one small step at a time. The psalmist made that evident in Psalm 119:105 where it states *Thy Word is a lamp unto my feet, and a light unto my pathway*. Even as the headlights on your car only have the capacity to shine light on the road for a few feet in front of you, so too does the instruction of God illuminate a small portion of your pathway. It's not that the Word and the Spirit of God are not capable of showing you more. The truth is, if God were to show us the fullness of His vision and plan for our lives it would likely frighten us into stagnation. Extraordinary leaders have the capacity to move one step and one directive at a time. It is possible to be doing so much that nothing gets done. Have you done the last thing that God was requiring of you to do?

I encourage you to take another look at the vision. Take a closer look at those things that God has instructed you to do. Disobedience to those things leads to the delay of the fulfillment of the vision. It is not coincidence that God created light before He created animals or man. There would have been utter chaos if animals or man had to maneuver in complete darkness. God works through order and systems. When you operate according to the order of God, you will experience the fullness of the vision being fulfilled in your life. Remember that He knows the end from the beginning. He knows how the vision is going to end. He has already established the outcome. It is important to lead by following.

MAKE THE NECESSARY ADJUSTMENTS

Never feel bad about making the necessary adjustments to fulfill what God has called you to fulfill. Success is a process, not a final destination. We achieve success one obedient act at a time. The road that you are on will lead you somewhere – the real question is will it lead you to the ultimate destiny that God has established in your life? There have been far too many occasions in my life that I have had to make major adjustments or even completely stop what I was doing when I realized that I was moving further away from God's original will and intent for my life.

A few years ago my wife and I moved from California to Texas with the intent to plant a church in that region. We came, we got settled in, and we got busy. That was a huge mistake. I hadn't taken the time to learn the lay of the land, I hadn't taken the time to learn the culture, and I hadn't taken the time to count the cost for starting ministry here. Eight months later, we opened the doors to our first church. Needless to say the church was never healthy, and it never grew. Why? Because I moved ahead of God's timing, and outside of His will. After months of going through the motions, I had to lay my pride aside and shut it down. The wonderful thing is that when I stood before the church to announce that we were shutting down, there was no push back. That could be because my wife and two sons were the only members of the church.

It is never a crime to get into the center of God's will. If what you are doing does not line up to the instruction that God has given you, stop it. If you are unclear about what God desires for you to do next, pray diligently and don't move until you have heard from Him. If you know for a fact that what you are doing is not in His will for your life, shut it down. You don't have the time or energy to operate in areas that are not divinely assigned to your life. God is never disappointed with your obedience.

You may even be experiencing great success in areas that God never predestined for you to be in. As an extraordinary leader, you are going to have to decide whether God's plan for your life is more important than your plans for your life. If what you are doing does not line up to God's purpose and plan for your life, adjust accordingly.

TAKE ACTION

1. Examine your heart. Is your heart bent towards God's plan and will for your life as a person? As a leader? Take an honest and written account of any personal agendas and then submit them to God.

2. Consider where you are in your journey – as a spouse, parent, entrepreneur, ministry leader. Are you confused regarding the next step that you should take? Write down the steps the Lord has instructed you to take so far and ensure that you've done those things.

3. What adjustments (if any) do you need to make to get realigned with the Lord's will for your life? Is there something you need to START doing? Is there something you need to STOP doing? Make a written commitment of the steps you'll take to re-align with His will.

Principle #6:
It's Lonely At The Top

"Extraordinary leadership is about having the patience to wait while the world around you catches up to what is in your heart."

"Don't you see it Micah? It's right there. That cloud that looks like a dragon." Micah responded with an enthusiastic "Where?" "Over there! The one that looks like a dragon with its mouth open", Zion quickly responded. "Oh. Now I see it", responded Micah. This was a conversation that my sons were having in the back seat of the car one day as I was taking them home from school. My oldest son Zion had seen what looked to him to resemble a dragon in the clouds, and he was attempting to help my youngest son Micah identify the same cloud that he'd seen. In all honesty, I am not certain that Micah ever really saw the cloud that Zion was referring to. I believe that in an attempt to relate to his brother (and his vision) he agreed that he had seen the dragon in the sky. What is even more interesting is that even while I was driving, I could look over and see the exact cloud that he was referring to. So what does this all mean for the extraordinary leader? I am glad that you asked.

Zion was doing what you may have done before. He was attempting to convince someone who did not have this vision or vantage point to recognize and identify a vision that he could not fully relate to.

As much as Micah wanted to see what Zion was seeing and saying, he couldn't. Why? There are two key things that made it difficult for Micah to see what Zion was seeing. The first thing is that there were literally 30 to 40 clouds surrounding the one particular cloud that Zion was referring to. The other problem was, although Micah has a very creative imagination, his imagination would not allow him to see in the cloud what Zion saw. There are a few things we can take away from this, as we challenge ourselves to operate in an extraordinary way:

1. *Not everyone who walks with you can see what you see.* Be careful not to allow yourself to get frustrated by people who don't grasp your vision right away. Remember, you are often asking them to become enthusiastic about your vision in five minutes when you have had the opportunity to live with this vision in your heart for days, months, or even years. Sometimes, extraordinary leadership is about having the patience to wait while the world around you catches up to what is in your heart.

2. *Never force someone to see things your way.* It's better to have someone who will support you without seeing the vision than to have someone who will spend all of their time and productivity trying to see the vision before they support the vision. If they are forced to lie at

the beginning, they we feel obligated to lie until the end. You have to accept the fact that sometimes you're the only one who will ever fully see the dragon in the clouds.

3. *Sometimes the problem isn't their vision, but rather it's your description.* One of the most valuable leadership lessons that I have learned is that people take their cues from you. They are confident in a leader who is confident in their own vision. If you aren't certain about the vision, you cannot expect anyone else to be. It is important that the extraordinary leader receive his own vision before he casts that vision.

4. *Your vision can be lost in translation.* As an extraordinary leader who is casting vision, you have to cast your vision in a language that the people around you understand. It doesn't matter how willing someone is to support your vision and to run with it, if you are speaking English and they speak Portuguese -- it is going to be quite difficult for them to receive what you are saying. While language barriers can be a problem, I am speaking more to the idea of making your vision clear, relatable, and easy to run with. People will support a vision when they find something in the vision the supports them. How does your vision help the people who you are asking to support it?

5. *Is it for you or is it for them?* Sometimes the dragons in the clouds are not for other people. Sometimes God uses those opportunities to stretch you, to expand your ability to dream, and to believe. Be careful about sharing every idea that you have with the people who are around you and particularly those who are following you. People lose trust in leaders who don't follow through with what they have said. Make sure that the vision that you are asking them to behold is one that you are planning on pursuing and seeing through to the end. One of the most frustrating things for vision supporters is to hear a visionary bring up ten brilliant ideas and to complete none of them. If you are going to point out the dragon in the sky, make sure that you are planning on doing something with the dragon in the sky.

6. *Don't be afraid to push people to see more.* Leadership is influence. There are many occasions that God will cause you to point out vision so that He can stretch the vision of those around you. There are many who won't believe that they can dream as big as they can until they have seen you point out the dragon in the sky. Leadership is about taking people from where they are now to where they never believed that they could go. You do this by casting vision, and then leading them through

the process of fulfilling the vision.

7. *Walk them through it.* If they are having a hard time seeing the dragon in the cloud, take them through the process slowly and methodically. Extraordinary leaders are leaders who practice patience. You cannot effectively lead people when you have no patience for people. Leadership takes patience, and patience takes prayer.

The moral of the story is this: Don't expect everyone to see what you see, feel what you feel, desire what you desire, or to chase after what you chase after. Ultimately, you may be the only person who ever really sees the dragon in the cloud. You have to be okay with that, and more importantly, you have to be okay with you. There are times as a leader and as a visionary that you feel like you are walking alone. It is in those moments that you must be confident that what you are seeing is what God is showing you, and that you will follow after that vision, by any means necessary.

LEADERSHIP LESSONS FROM THE ELEVATOR

One afternoon while I was at work and about to step on an elevator, the Lord began dealing with me concerning leadership. Before I share what He downloaded into my spirit, let me give you the backdrop. On this particular day, it was a time of day where there was a lot of traffic on the elevators. It wouldn't be uncommon to have to wait for five minutes or longer for one elevator. As you can probably guess, there were quite a few people, many of whom were friends of colleagues of mine who were gathering and waiting on an elevator as well. As the elevator arrived and the doors opened, the crowd of people who were in the elevator exited, and those of us who were waiting in eager anticipation for the elevator crowded on. We all pressed the button to our designated destinations, and as the elevator began going up, individuals exited on their preferred floor. I had been on this elevator hundreds of times before, but I had never heard the Lord minister to me like He did on this particular day, and at that particular moment. Here are a few leadership lessons that I learned on the way up:

Leadership Lesson #1: Not everyone who starts out with you will finish with you.

Even as I started out with the crowd in the basement of that building, when I reached my final destination on the sixth floor, there were only a few people left that I'd started out with. Don't be alarmed when people who you thought would go the distance with you, and who would be there when the full vision comes into fruition, walk out of your life.

Leadership Lesson #2: Not everyone who walks into your life is on your level.

What do I mean? There were some people who got on the elevator on the third floor, and exited on the fourth floor. Some people are only along for a short season. Be careful not to run the guilt trip on people when they leave prematurely. They aren't necessarily on your level, which is not a bad thing.

Leadership Lesson #3: They may smile in your face and turn their back on you.

There were people who walked into the elevator after me and greeted me with a smile. What is interesting is that when they found a safe and comfortable position in the elevator, they turned their back towards me. I heard the Lord say that on your journey up, there will always be someone that smiles with you on the way up, but they will eventually turn their back on you, and at some point even walk out of your life. That doesn't make you any less of a leader.

Leadership Lesson #4: Never settle for a level that is not assigned to your life.

When God gives you a vision, He intends to fulfill that vision through you. It would have been easy for me to exit on a floor that was not mine simply to be around people who I enjoyed being around, but I had somewhere to be. I had a purpose to fulfill. As extraordinary leaders, it is important that we not settle in a place that is not in our sphere of influence. Live and lead on your own level.

Leadership Lesson#5: People will push your buttons.

Leadership is about patience and tolerance. It is about forgiveness and integrity. What is interesting is that although someone else pushed the number six before me in the elevator, it led me to my final destination. When you submit your attitude to the will of the Lord for your life, God will use the "button pushers" in your life, the people that irritate you the most, to push you to your destiny.

Leadership Lesson#6: Not everyone who stands with you is familiar with you.

The elevator that we were on was crowded. There were people I was standing next to who I had never seen in my life yet we were headed in the same direction. Be careful about how you treat the strangers that walk into your life. You never know who will be willing to go the distance with you.

Leadership Lesson#7: Celebrate your progress.

As I was on the elevator I watched the floor numbers change and each change symbolized the fact that I was one step closer to my destination. That's how it should be with us as leaders! You must celebrate your progress, and you cannot celebrate with your head down. It is vital that leaders remain aware and engaged. Leadership is about the small steps that lead to giant breakthrough. Remember to always acknowledge where you started, and how far you have come from that moment.

Leadership Lesson #8: You can go down just as quickly as you went up.

Nobody wants to follow an arrogant self-centered leader. Proverbs 16:18 reminds us that pride goes before destruction, a high and mighty spirit before a fall. Be mindful that no matter how far God takes you, and no matter how high He allows you to go, you are one arrogant heartbeat away from being lower than where you've started. Remain humble.

Extraordinary leadership is never about forcing your way in. It has nothing to do with proving yourself to anyone. Extraordinary leadership has everything to do with following after what God has required of you to do and being a blessing to everyone you connect with on your journey up. In many cases, success as a leader is not just about how you handle the people in your life who benefit you, but also how you handle those people you come into contact with who do not benefit you at all. If you lead long enough, you will undoubtedly confront those scenarios, and those type of people. The extraordinary leader is the one who maintains godly character regardless of what the scenario is and who is involved.

OPINIONS...EVERYONE'S GOT ONE

I think what I admire most about Zack and his audacity in Luke 19:1-10 is that he never wasted time asking people for their opinion. He never got permission to audaciously go ahead of the crowd, or climb boldly into the sycamore tree. He just did it. Perhaps he understood that his actions were time sensitive, and he didn't want to miss his moment. It could also be that he was aware that what he was about to do was going to make him look like an idiot to those around him. He never allowed his movements to be predicated on whether people thought what he was doing was a good idea or not. He moved with all bravery toward his purpose, and it paid off in the end.

Are you waiting on someone to give you permission to be yourself? Are you looking for someone to approve the enormous vision that God has placed in you? While we are to always seek godly counsel, when it is all said and done, there are only two opinions that will ever matter concerning your vision. You need to know that God has approved you for this assignment, and God needs to know that your faith is strong enough for Him to pull it off through you. Everyone else's opinion is optional. Seek the Lord about what His desires are and follow after those desires.

While we are on the subject of opinions, I must point out that it is quite possible for your enemy to have more faith in your success than you have. It is difficult to fulfill a vision that you don't believe in, and even more difficult to be the one who fulfills it when you don't believe in yourself. Be sure that you are sold on the thing that you are called to do. It's tough enough to have to walk alone while you are fulfilling vision, but to have to do it when you don't even believe in yourself or the vision is an even more taxing situation to be in. Hold fast to the God who called you to lead, and trust that He will fulfill the vision that He has given you to fulfill. Sometimes that greatest weapon to vision is your opinion of yourself, and people's opinion of you.

TAKE ACTION

1. Write out the vision that you need to cast to those who are following you – this could be your family, your employees, your partners, and the people in your ministry. Use plain language that is easily understood and emphasizes how the vision helps those who you're seeking support from.

2. Celebrate the progress you're making in your journey. Start a journal that tracks the growth in the areas you're leading. Take note of how God showed up. Take note of how the people responded. Capture even the disappointing moments for the benefit of reflection and future growth.

Principle# 7:
Giving Your All

"Extraordinary leadership is more concerned with the people than it is with the plans."

One afternoon while I was walking through a parking lot, I saw a bumper sticker that not only grabbed my attention, but it tugged at my heart strings. The bumper sticker read "All gave some, but some gave all". The bumper sticker was patriotic in theme, and it featured an American flag in the background. By the look of the other bumper stickers on this particular vehicle, this person was a war veteran. Reading that bumper sticker caused me to reflect on the fact that if you have experienced any kind of military combat at all, you have given something. It also led me to consider the fact that there are people who enlisted in the armed forces voluntarily, went on a mission to defend their country, and never made it home from war. They died on the battlefield. If there were ever a clear cut example of what leadership looked like, that would be it.

There has never been and will never be a person who epitomizes leadership more than Christ Himself. Here is a man who left Heaven to come to earth for the sole purpose of dying for a people who did not deserve that kind of love. Consider that. He showed up to die. He came to be crucified. His sole purpose in the earth was death, and at an early age.

That, my friend, is leadership. No, I am not saying that leadership is about death. What I am saying is that leadership is about giving your all. If we are going to use Christ as our example of what ultimate leadership looks like, what we are really saying is that our purpose is the well-being of others. Can I prove it?

John 3:16, the most famous and most quoted scripture of all time reads, *For God loved the world so much that He gave His one and only son, so that whoever believes in Him will not perish but have life eternal.* This is the ultimate leadership scripture, as it highlights the mission of the Ultimate Leader, and His response to that mission. There are two things in the passage of scripture that I believe every leader needs to draw from. If there are two things that every extraordinary leader must master, it's love and giving. How can anyone lead at their maximum potential without having a love for the people who they are leading? According to this particular text, God's leadership was walked out in love, and His response to that love was to give. He didn't just love the people who would follow Him, but rather, He loved the world which included those who hated Him. He didn't just give His son for the people who loved Him, but He gave His son for the people who would eventually kill Him as well.

What does that say about what it means to be an extraordinary leader? It is not enough to hold a position, or even to have people following you. God has called you to a higher standard of leadership. You are called to lead with love. You are called to freely give as a response to love.

There was a time when I went on a bit of a rant about how many of the people I am ministering don't attend our church. I was complaining about the fact that most of these people had churches that they were very active in, and pastors who they had relationship with, yet they were coming to me for counsel and a better understanding of the Word of God. In my selfishness, I complained about being used by them. There is only one problem with that; God gave His all for all. His love doesn't have an RSVP section, or a VIP section. He simply loves, and He leads with love. I was convicted and relieved at the same time. I was convicted because of the selfishness that I was attempting to lead in, while in the same breath saying that I am a disciple of Christ. I was equally convicted about the fact that I was only willing to give to those who were in my VIP section. Shame on me.

People will always be more important than the vision will ever be. God gave you the vision for the people; He didn't give you the people for the vision. God desires to love the people through your vision, yet we often make the mistake of thinking that the people are created to love the vision. That is an arrogant frame of mind fueled by pride, and it is not the will of God. Please know that extraordinary leadership is more concerned with the people than it is with the plans. Remember, Christ came to the earth from Heaven to give. Whatever you and I do, we should do it with all of our might.

THE PERFECT LEADER

I recall my early days of ministry when I would mark some of the other men and women in ministry who were so much further ahead than I was. I began to dress like them, talk like them, and even pattern my preaching/teaching style after theirs. For all intents and purposes, I was trying to become them because obviously what they were doing was working. This worked for me for a while, and I was able to get away with this for a short time, until people who didn't know Christ would begin asking me all of these biblical questions that I had no answer to. Instead of admitting that I didn't know the answer or that I would research that question and respond later, I would simply make things up. What kind of leader makes things up?

Because I was young and untrained, I assumed that people were looking for a perfect leader. I thought that they were looking for someone who could look the part, play the part, and always have the perfect answers. I was an accident waiting to happen. What I later discovered is that people are not looking for a leader who is perfect; they are looking for a leader who is authentic. They are looking for a person who they can relate to, and who they can trust to be transparent while still maintaining their character. Consider the fact that Jesus spent most of His time with imperfect people. Although He was perfect, His humanity and compassion for them made Him relatable and trustworthy. His compassion allowed Him to meet them where they were, and to lead them to where they needed to be. It was the religious legalists who had a problem with Jesus, not the imperfect sinners. Jesus' transparency was the key that allowed Him to unlock the hearts of so many who He came into contact with.

God knew that you and I were imperfect before He called us to lead. Extraordinary leaders embrace who they are, they embrace who they are not, and they use both to their advantage to lead people to their destiny. Spending time pretending to be who you are not is time taken from operating in the fullness of who you are. People know that you aren't perfect. They don't expect you to be perfect. To pretend that you are perfect is selling yourself short of the thing that makes you an exceptional leader in the first place. They will follow you because they see something in you that speaks to them. If you are hiding behind the facade of perfection, they will never experience the true leader in you, and you will never be able to pull on their greatest potential. Transparency is key.

In Luke 19, Zack's imperfection led to his greatest moment of innovation. It was the thing that literally drove him up a tree. You would be surprised by the doors and opportunities that are waiting to be opened to you once you confront your imperfections and allow God to navigate you as a leader. Consider David, Moses, Paul, Abraham, Elijah, and countless other imperfect extraordinary leaders in the Bible who God chose to use to manifest His will. God didn't choose them because they were perfect. He chose them because they weren't. You are no different. You don't have to be perfect to be an extraordinary leader; you just have to be willing.

BE THE CURE

Working in the medical field for years, I have seen countless things change in medicine. One of the things that has changed is that now, in most hospitals, the flu shot is mandatory for employment. I was okay with the flu shot until I discovered that they are actually injecting me with another form of the influenza (flu) virus. Did you get that? The anti-virus is the virus. In essence, the very thing that strengthens your immune system against the flu is the flu. I can imagine that by now you are wondering what in the world this has to do with leadership, so allow me to explain.

Leadership is ministry. When you minister from your weaknesses, you will always have an audience. When you lead from your brokenness, you will always have someone who is willing to follow you. People need to know that they can relate to you. Every negative experience that you have been through was training for your defining moment as a person, and as an extraordinary leader. You are someone's influenza vaccine. You are the cure to someone's diseased heart. This is why it is vitally important that you allow yourself to lead from a place of transparency and even brokenness. Your compassion for others will flow through your ability to understand them as an individual.

You haven't gone through what you have gone through for nothing. God has placed you in the earth as a response to a void that needs to be filled. Your experiences, your failures, your setbacks, your dropped balls, and your screw ups are all fuel for the fire that God designed to burn in you as an extraordinary leader. Don't apologize for who you are or for what you have had to go through to be here. You may be reading this while you are presently in a storm. That storm doesn't make you any less of leader; it makes you more of an extraordinary leader. You can't go through what you have gone through and not be extraordinary.

I pray that you discover the problem in the earth that you were designed to solve. I pray that you discover the emotional disease that you were created to be the cure for. Your extraordinary gift and leadership is not in what you have or have not done in the past, but rather about what you will and will not do in the future. Don't ask for the lead, take the lead. Be the cure.

TAKE ACTION

Reflect on how you lead.
1. Are you leading with love? What are some areas where you can increase the level of love that you show towards those you're leading?

2. Are you leading authentically? What are some of the experiences you've had in your life (past or present) that can serve as a benefit to those you serve? There is power in your story.

Conclusion

To me, one of the highlights of flying is when the pilot makes the announcement of "Ladies and Gentlemen – We have been cleared for takeoff." This means that all traffic on land and above has been cleared, and that there is nothing that can hinder the flight from taking off. I want to take this opportunity to make an announcement on the intercom of your heart by informing you that ***you have been cleared for takeoff!*** The extraordinary leader in you has been given clearance to soar.

The odds are that you have chosen to read this book because you are either already aware of your leadership potential, or you feel like there may be a leader in you that has not been actualized. I pray that by now you are very clear about the fact that everyone is called to lead in some capacity. I also pray that as you have read this book, you have a better understanding of how to take that "some capacity", to the next level of leadership. You are an extraordinary leader, and the world is waiting to experience it. You have exactly what it takes to live, love, and lead on a new level. I absolutely believe in the "Zack" in you. As I close this book out, I want to invite you to pray a prayer with me for the release of the extraordinary leader that is within you.

Repeat this prayer:

Holy Spirit, thank You for choosing me before the foundations of the earth. Thank You that I am fearfully and wonderfully made. Thank You Lord that I am the head and not the tail, above only and not beneath. Thank You that although I make mistakes, I am not a mistake. Thank you that I haven't stumbled into leadership, but that I am called to leadership.

Lord, I receive and embrace a new dimension of leadership today. I declare that the extraordinary leader that I am now has full permission to think, act, and speak on my behalf. Help me to lead in faith and not fear. Give me the courage to take the limitations off of my capabilities as a leader. I celebrate you today for choosing me for such a time as this. Lord, if you will do the navigating, I will do the leading.

In Jesus' name I pray. Amen.

About The Author

David A. Burrus was born in Berkeley, California in 1975. While he has lived in many places and experienced many cultures, he now calls Hewitt, Texas his home. Having much academia and the strong belief in advancement through education, Mr. Burrus intends to continue his studies to eventually earn a Doctoral Degree in Psychology. His wife, Tanisha L. Burrus is an entrepreneur and serves as executive director of David A. Burrus Global and DB | 475. David and Tanisha have two sons, Zion and Micah-Israel.

Today, David is a pastor, teacher, administrator, author, motivational speaker, entrepreneur, and philanthropist. He does a great deal of traveling as a speaker addressing leaders, businesses, schools/universities and church congregations. He personally addresses thousands of people each year on personal and professional development. He is the author of "The Blueprint: Discovering God's Intent for Relationships", as well as the founder of The Passion Summit Relationship Institute.

David places a great emphasis on the Kingdom of God and believes that the whole Bible, along with the message of Jesus, revolved around the Kingdom and not a religion. He has said, "My vision as a leader is to get people from where they are to where they have never been."

Bonus Online Resources

Leadership and Relationship Insights from a Kingdom Perspective:
DavidABurrus.com

Weekly e-zine, Kingdom Impact:
KingdomDrivenEntrepreneur.com

The Kingdom Driven Entrepreneur Podcast
KingdomDrivenEntrepreneur.com
Subscribe via iTunes or Stitcher Radio today!

Other Books for Kingdom Driven Entrepreneurs

The Kingdom Driven Entrepreneur: Doing Business God's Way (ISBN: 978-0615736129)

The Kingdom Driven Entrepreneur's Guide To Goal Setting (ISBN: 978-0615771892)

The Kingdom Driven Entrepreneur's Guide To Fearless Business Finance (ISBN: 978-0989632201)

The Kingdom Driven Entrepreneur's Guide To Holistic Health (ISBN: 978-0989632218)

Encountering God: A Devotional for the Kingdom Driven Entrepreneur (ISBN: 978-0989632225)

www.ingramcontent.com/pod-product-compliance
Lightning Source LLC
Chambersburg PA
CBHW061505040426
42450CB00008B/1487